CLASSIC MARQUES

Hillman Cars
1945-1964

MALCOLM BOBBITT

NOSTALGIA ROAD

A CIP record for this book is available from
the British Library

ISBN 9 781908 347015

Printed in Malta by Melita Press

Crécy Publishing Limited
1a Ringway Trading Estate
Shadowmoss Road
Manchester M22 5LH

www.crecy.co.uk

Front Cover: The Hillman Imp Mark II. *Rootes publicity/
author's collection*

Rear Cover Top: A 1954 Minx Mk VIII under scrutiny.
Rootes publicity/Alan Earnshaw collection.
Bottom: Front detail of 1936 Minx Tourer. *Author*

Contents Page: The Hillman Minx was produced over a
period of some 45 years, the model being announced
first in 1931 and entering production the following
year. Illustrated is a Series III Minx convertible, this
version being announced in September 1958 and
remaining in production until 1961. *Author*

Acknowledgements

THE author is grateful to the following people who have helped to make this
publication possible. In addition to photographs from the author's collection, a
number of others are from the collection of the late Professor Alan Earnshaw, who
allowed me to access his collection from the Rootes Group archives. Motoring
historian and researcher Andrew Minney supplied both photographic material as
well as road test documents while Martin Bourne and Richard Mann provided much
useful background material and technical information. My grateful thanks are due
also to Nigel Stennett-Cox for going through my manuscript and putting me right
on various issues. Not least, my grateful thanks go to Jon Day at the National Motor
Museum Photographic Department, and to Reg Barker and others for allowing me
to photograph their Hillmans.

CONTENTS

Introduction

Hillman is one of the best-remembered names in British motoring history but, like many of its contemporaries, has fallen into obscurity. As with other names that are now mere memories, Hillman was at the birth of the motor industry having evolved from bicycle making. It was in Coventry in the second half of the 19th century where William Hillman set up business and, with James Starley, patented the Aerial bicycle. Those formative years were crucial as they were the beginnings of not only the Hillman car but also, via the Starley family, Rover.

The first Hillman car appeared in 1907 and was known as a Hillman-Coatalen in acknowledgement of the vehicle's designer. The company developed cautiously and it wasn't until World War 1 that it saw expansion. Nevertheless, by the mid- to late-1920s, Hillman's finances were somewhat shaky and production accounted for fewer than 5,000 cars annually despite the name being an assurance of quality and reliability. Hillman's fragility became the springboard for the Rootes brothers, already a force in the motor trade as distributor of Austin cars throughout London and the Home Counties, to expand into vehicle manufacturing. Under Rootes' ownership, not only did Hillman eventually become one of Britain's most important and familiar names, it shared a place within a mighty and hugely successful empire encompassing such revered names as Humber, Singer, Sunbeam and Sunbeam-Talbot as well as the coachbuilding firm of Thrupp & Maberly.

The intention of this book is to study the Hillman years from the immediate post-war period to the mid-1960s, an age when these cars were a familiar sight not only on British roads but those around the world. This is the era of the Minx, one of the most revered family cars, and its siblings the chic Californian and hard working Husky. The Hillman range was extended with the arrival of the Super Minx and by the debut of the Imp, which was a revolutionary small car that would, it was hoped, rival the Mini. This book also takes a look at the later generation of Hillmans that were the marque's swansong as well as the final years of the Rootes' business.

Often perceived as being conservative family cars, Hillmans were never far away from the sporting scene. The Minx participated in some of the most gruelling rallies, including the Monte Carlo, and the Imp also emerged as a formidable rally competitor.

Malcolm Bobbitt
Cockermouth, 2011

the finest of them all!

The American design consultant Raymond Loewy was enlisted post-war to advise Rootes on styling issues. Thus the Series 1 Minx portrayed here evinces some similarity with the Studebaker, with which Loewy was also associated. This publicity item is a charming period piece carrying an essential 'feel good' factor. *Rootes publicity/Author's collection*

Under Rootes' control Hillman was always at the forefront of technology, in this instance the column-mounted Synchromatic gear change that allowed supposedly effortless fingertip control of the Minx's four-speed crash-proof gearbox. *Rootes advert in* The Motor/*Author's collection*

Despite the Minx's outward appearance as a staid family car, it was, nevertheless, a frequent motor sport contender. This Series I Minx was pictured at Goodwood on 31 August 1957 when taking part in a BARC event. *National Motor Museum*

It's a great change!

HILLMAN MINX

A CAR WITH A GREAT PAST . . . AND A GREAT FUTURE

A PRODUCT OF THE ROOTES GROUP

5

The Rootes' Empire

H ILLMAN was just one of several car manufacturing companies that were part of a company — the Rootes Group — that also included Humber, Singer, Sunbeam and Sunbeam-Talbot. Rootes was not only about car-making as the firm had other interests, including vehicle sales and distribution. It was also involved in coachbuilding through the acquisition of Thrupp & Maberly.

The origins of the Rootes' empire can be traced to the late 19th century when William Rootes owned a cycle shop at Hawkhurst in Kent. William had two sons, William Edward, born 1894 and known as Billy, and Reginald Claud, born 1896.

As with many business people who were involved in the bicycle industry, William's interests turned to the motorcar and it wasn't long before he opened a motor agency in Hawkhurst, which, at the onset of war in 1914, was selling a wide variety of cars. After the war, Billy and Reginald joined forces to establish Rootes Ltd, the necessary finance to set up in business having come from their father with a gift of £2,400. Billy was the driving force in the partnership, always full of ideas and on the look-out for a business opportunity; Reginald was the calm administrator who ensured that the firm kept an even keel.

Soon after Rootes Distributors was formed in the early 1920s, the company assumed responsibility for Austin distribution in London and the Home Counties. Then followed interests in the Midlands-based garage chain George Heath and in the Manchester operation of Tom Garner. In addition it bought out the London-based motor dealership Warwick Wright in 1928. It was through the entrepreneurial efforts of Billy and Reginald that the brothers became the largest and most successful car distributors in Britain. By far the most impressive business venture was the purchase of Thrupp & Maberly whose coachwork was regarded as being of particularly high quality. Under Rootes' control Thrupp & Maberly's prestige was enhanced, the coachbuilder's products being considered as being among the very best the British coachbuilding industry could offer, the same coachbuilder being responsible for a number of bespoke bodies fitted to Rolls-Royce, Bentley, Daimler and other marques as well as the body of Sir Henry Segrave's 1929 Land Speed Record contender *Golden Arrow*. Its expertise was also applied to Humber when Rootes acquired the marque and, during World War 2, the coachbuilder was responsible for the construction of Humber staff cars.

Another significant move was to install the Rootes' headquarters within the prestigious and newly erected Devonshire House, opposite the Ritz Hotel in London's Piccadilly. By establishing themselves in what *The Autocar* referred to as magnificent showrooms, the Rootes brothers took the motor industry by storm.

It had always been Billy Rootes' aim to enter the car manufacturing business but, when the opportunity arose to acquire Standard in the 1920s, negotiations faltered. Another chance to take control of an established car-maker came in the second half of the 1920s when the then ailing Hillman firm sought a merger with neighbouring Humber, which was also experiencing financial difficulties.

The merger of Hillman and Humber, along with the commercial vehicle firm Commer, was reported in *The Autocar* in 1928, after which Rootes' influence was already apparent in so much as the firm was fully in charge of Hillman, Humber and Commer's export activities. By 1929 the three vehicle manufacturers were incorporated within the Rootes' empire, with brothers Billy and Reginald comfortably at the helm of the business. Billy's dream of creating a manufacturing empire much in the idiom of General Motors was, in his view, well on the way to fruition. His aspirations in this respect were boosted when Rootes Securities Ltd, having invested in Sunbeam-Talbot-Darracq (STD), took over the British interests of the combine in 1935 following evidence of STD's financial position and its inability to meet loan repayments.

The Rootes brothers, having acquired Hillman in 1929, introduced the Hillman Wizard in January 1930. Billy Rootes was responsible for a spectacular event in which a pre-production example was driven from Britain to the heat and sands of North Africa, thus convincing the Metropolitan Police to use the model for police work. A Wizard 65 is seen here with its police crew soon after its acquisition by the Metropolitan Police. *Metropolitan Police Museum*

The second Rootes Hillman to be developed was the Minx, which was designed by Captain Irving and A. H. Wilde, the latter having devised the Standard 9. When it was shown at the 1931 Paris Salon, the Minx was well received. The saloon depicted here was built in 1934. *Author*

In addition to saloons, the Minx range comprised a four-seat open tourer and, after 1934, a streamlined open two-seater. This beautifully represented four-seat tourer dates from 1936 and features a four-speed all-synchromesh gearbox. *Author*

The Hillman insignia under Rootes' ownership was synonymous with quality and value for money. The cars had channel section frames, rear half-elliptic springs and Bendix cable-operated brakes. A feature was 'cushion power', which allowed engines to rock on flexible rubber blocks for smooth running. *Author*

Under the direction of the Rootes brothers, Hillman was totally reorganised and the Coventry factory refitted to facilitate a large increase in output to challenge the mass-production methods of Morris. Humber, too, underwent reorganisation and, whilst that firm became identified with luxury cars, it was left to Hillman to satisfy the more popular market with family models that were keenly priced.

Hillman, like so many fledgling carmakers, evolved through bicycle making. William Hillman had left his native London in favour of Coventry, which was the centre of the cycle industry, and it is there he went into partnership with another bicycle maker, James Starley. The latter was the force behind the firm that was to produce eventually the Rover and, later, the car of the same name. William Hillman's first car was the 1907 Hillman-Coatalen but it wasn't until 1913 with the introduction of the 1,327cc Nine that the company enjoyed any degree of success. After World War 1 Hillman won recognition with the Speed model, which proved to be a worthy contender at Brooklands. Its sporting potential was assured with some good performances on behalf of Hillman's works driver, George Bedford, and a young racing driver by the name of Raymond Mays.

The mainstay of Hillman production during the early 1920s was the rugged and reliable 11 and 14hp models. Output was never anything but modest and the firm's shaky financial position was the factor that attracted the Rootes brothers' attention.

When the Hillman Minx was introduced in 1931, several months after the Wizard, the first new car under Rootes' ownership, it not only filled a gap in the 10hp vehicle market, it became a best-seller and was responsible for Rootes emerging as a leading British car manufacturer.

The Minx was an all-new car, which, being smaller and cheaper than previous Hillmans, spearheaded the Rootes' range. Despite being perceived as a mass-produced economy car — which it was — the Minx was well received by none other than W. O. Bentley, the builder of famous sports cars who was invited to put the car through its paces prior to introduction. The opportunity for Bentley to try the Minx came at the time of Bentley Motors' financial collapse and subsequent acquisition by Rolls-Royce. Bentley was without a job and a car, so the invitation from Billy Rootes was as much a gesture of friendship as well as a genuine desire to have the car properly evaluated. Though the Wizard, with a choice of six-cylinder 2.1 and 2.8 litre engines (65 and 75 respectively), was included in the model line-up, it was the Minx that, over successive generations, became the Rootes' market leader.

When they were introduced in 1931, both models of Wizards were sufficiently tough to be used for police work. After 1933 the Wizard name was dropped, the 65 being rebadged as the 16hp, and the 75 the 20-70. These models in turn gave way to entirely new cars in 1935 featuring larger engines and modified chassis with independent front suspension.

The larger Hillmans — 16hp, Hawk and 80 — were more akin to Humbers and remained in production until 1937. Thereafter, the smaller models, up to 14hp, were marketed as Hillmans and the larger cars as Humbers. It was the 14hp that was the most powerful Hillman in the Rootes' catalogue prior to the outbreak of war in 1939.

Right: The Minx Magnificent was introduced for the 1936 model year and cost £159. It was larger and heavier than the original car, though its mechanical specification remained largely as before. By 1939 some 90,000 Magnificents had been built. *Author's collection*

The Metropolitan Police purchased a fleet of Minx Tourers for traffic duties. This 1934 photograph depicts a driver training session calling for a Le Mans type start. *Metropolitan Police Museum*

For Rootes, the Hillman Minx was the 'bread and butter' model and the car that appeared in 1931 was of straightforward design. Having half-elliptic springs front and rear, cable-operated brakes, a side-valve engine and a three-speed crash gearbox, all of which were built upon a channel-section chassis, it provided uncomplicated motoring at a purchase price of £159. For the money, buyers got a comfortable and reliable vehicle fitted with a Pressed Steel body, the type of which was specified for a number of British cars of the era.

Tough competition from other British manufacturers forced Rootes to improve the Minx so that, within two years, the car displayed such improvements as a four-speed gearbox and freewheel device, both of which were optional over the basic model. Then came a styling facelift for 1934, the revised model having a raked radiator and semaphore indicators. It was the 1936 Minx that was distinctively different from earlier models: not only was the body restyled so that it afforded more comfortable accommodation, the car was heavier than its predecessors and featured a modified box section chassis frame. Mechanically the new car was similar to its predecessor, the established 1,185cc engine producing 30bhp at 4,100rpm, which, jointly with the Ford, was the most powerful family 'Ten'. Rootes decided that the new Minx, which shared styling similarities with its Humber sibling, should have a name that reflected a bright, new, and young image, hence the Minx Magnificent was born.

The Wizard's replacement was the Hillman Hawk; the example recorded here is pictured in police service. Hawks had six-cylinder engines and were technically more akin to Humber models. *Metropolitan Police Museum*

Soon after the Minx had appeared, Rootes introduced the Aero Minx, a sports version of the car, though its performance was only marginally improved over that of the saloon courtesy of a high compression cylinder head. It was the Aero's rakish shape, the work of Georges Roesch whose services had been secured as part of the Sunbeam-Talbot-Darracq deal, which set the car apart from the standard Minx. The appealing design was enhanced by some striking coachwork styles, some of which emanated from Thrupp & Maberly, but it was only a matter of time before this attractive tourer with centre-lock wire wheels was rebadged as a Talbot 10 for the 1936 model year.

The Minx Magnificent remained in production until 1939, by which time an entirely new model, featuring a monocoque bodyshell, had been devised in readiness for the 1940 model year. During its span of production, the Minx Magnificent was mainly specified for Pressed Steel saloon coachwork though a number of other body styles, including a four-seat drophead coupé, were specified in the catalogue. Improvements to the car had been implemented in 1937 — the year that witnessed the building of the 100,000th Minx — these being chiefly limited to the frontal styling and provision of an externally accessed luggage compartment. Of the few technical revisions that were introduced, the most significant was a seemingly retrograde step in that first-gear synchromesh on the car's four-speed gearbox was deleted.

The decision to proceed with a monocoque car was taken in light of chassis developments elsewhere in the motor industry. Billy Rootes, who was fond of visiting the USA (sufficiently, it is said, to give him a voluntary American accent), would have known that Morris Motors, along with General Motors' British subsidiary Vauxhall, had decided to pursue the chassisless design of body construction and, in this respect, he was determined to be at the forefront of this technology. By the mid-1930s Rootes had become a formidable force within the British car industry and, at the time of the outbreak of war in 1939, was fully established as one of the country's 'big six' manufacturers with annual output of 50,000 vehicles.

The introduction of the monocoque Minx in September 1939 was overshadowed by Britain's commitment to war. Badged as the Hillman Minx Phase I, the new model appeared to be very similar to its predecessor and it was only the grille, with its 'alligator' bonnet and boot bulge, that immediately differentiated it from the Minx Magnificent. Both cars shared overall dimensions and a 7ft 8in wheelbase and, in

Seen here with the addition of wartime white paint (designed to improve visibility during the black out), the Hillman 14 was, from 1937, the largest of the Hillman models. Powered by a 1,944cc four-cylinder engine of Humber derivation, the 14 was fitted with the all-synchromesh Minx gearbox. *Metropolitan Police Museum*

Pictured *circa* 1957, this scene depicts a Metropolitan Police road safety campaign. The Minx wears a 1936 registration while the Wolseley behind it carries a 1948 plate. This was the era when police visited schools to perform daring stunts aimed at making children aware of road and traffic dangers. *Metropolitan Police Museum*

keeping with its forerunner's technical simplicity, the Phase I Minx continued to be powered by the faithful 1,185cc four-cylinder engine. This unit, at 35bhp and 4,100rpm, had an excellent output for a side-valve 10, producing slightly more power than previous models.

Though the new Hillman Minx was not the first British car to feature unitary construction, Billy Rootes could at least take much satisfaction that the car was indeed only the third so to do and, therefore, was instrumental in demonstrating his vehicles to be of the most modern design.

Owing to the start of hostilities, most would-be customers, apart from essential users, had to wait until the resumption of car manufacturing post-war before there was any hope of buying the Phase 1. Even then, the purchase of new cars was made very difficult as a result of the need to export most of Britain's car output. Whilst examples of the monocoque Phase I Minx were made available during the war to essential users, such as doctors and midwives, the majority of vehicles that were built were Utilities destined for war work and the armed forces. By the end of 1942 output had reached in excess of 10,000 vehicles and, therefore, shared a place in history with Austin's 8 and 10 Utilities.

Before the war, Rootes responded at an early date to the British government's call to the motor industry to help equip the country's armed forces through the shadow factory scheme. Resources were therefore partially diverted to assemble aircraft, aero engines, various military components and ammunition, armoured cars and vehicles that were imported from America in knocked-down form. In addition a huge number of Minxes and Humber Super Snipes were constructed for the war effort, the total amounting to 11 per cent of Britain's wartime vehicle output.

Hillman Minxes produced for the war effort at home and abroad were highly regarded for their rugged construction and reliability. Some were designed to run on town gas owing to petrol shortages, others were employed as staff cars while a number were sent to France to supplement General de Gaulle's Free French forces. Hillman was only a relatively small part of the Rootes' realm, a group that in wartime did much to bolster the resources of the armed forces. Not only did Rootes administer factories throughout the country, when the city of Coventry was devastated by enemy bombing on the night of 14 November 1940, it was Billy Rootes who was made chairman of the city's reconstruction and co-ordinating committee. Later Billy chaired the Supply Council of the Ministry of Supply with such effectiveness that his efforts were rewarded with a knighthood in the 1942 New Year Honours List. Reginald Rootes, too, was equally active in helping with the war effort, for which he was also to receive a knighthood.

When the war ended Rootes was not only in a healthy position financially, the company was well placed to resume car production, particularly as, in common with other car makers, the shadow factories allotted to them in the interests of the war effort, allowed for ideal manufacturing facilities. Billy Rootes, who pre-war had been instrumental in establishing overseas markets for his cars, was favourably placed to respond to and take advantage of the call to build as many vehicles as possible for export.

In the mid-1930s Dutch rally driver Maurice Gatsonides participated in the Monte Carlo Rally with his Hillman Minx. The car is seen here fitted with a rudimentary snowplough to get him through snow drifts. *Hans Berends*

The Minx Era

WHEN car production resumed post-war, Rootes enjoyed as good a position as it was possible to be in. Work undertaken during wartime for the British government had produced a healthy financial position and, moreover, the company's factories had emerged from the hostilities mainly unscathed. This meant that production of civilian cars was able to get under way in 1945, though there had been little time in which to develop any new models.

The first Hillman to appear post-war was the monocoque Phase I Minx. This was a dependable car that was made even more reliable by virtue of the fact that wartime models built for military purposes and for use by essential users provided Rootes' engineers with much valuable information. Any weak points that were evident when the car was introduced pre-war were eradicated and, according to Rootes' publicity material released in July 1945, the post-war model featured as many as 50 improvements. The new Minx not only benefited from improved fuel economy, it also demonstrated a swifter cruising speed, smoother running and a useful 5bhp increase in power. With its separate headlamps and pre-war styling, the Minx by 1947 standards was showing its age, but that did not deter Rootes from embarking upon a marketing campaign using a series of evocative advertisements, the message being 'It's good to look back...but even better to look forward'. Naturally, in the advertising style of the time, which aimed at looking beyond the restrictions that austerity presented, the messages that were put across to hopeful car buyers were far rosier than was the case.

At the beginning of 1947 Lockheed introduced a new development in hydraulic braking that saw the use of two leading shoes and twin wheel cylinders fitted to the front wheels, along with leading and trailing shoes in the rear drums, and it was this arrangement that was specified for the Minx later that year. This was in advance of the Phase II Minx, which was unveiled the following December. The new model designation was significant due to the technical modifications and the car's new frontal shape.

In achieving a new look for the Minx, Hillman designers had modified the alligator bonnet so that it featured more rounded shoulders and no longer carried the grille. The latter itself was somewhat narrowed in shape to emphasise the horizontal line. Most obvious about the re-styling were the reshaped front wings with integrated headlamps and the v-section bumper, which, as well as having a recess for the number plate, had a neat in-fill valance. The overall effect was modern and attractive while affording some mild Americanisation. Other than re-sculpturing the front of the car, which masked the familiar 1,185cc side-valve four, the Minx's body styling was, nonetheless, left-over from the Phase I.

An all-new monocoque Minx, known as the Phase I, was revealed in the autumn of 1939. As a result of the onset of war only a few of the cars found their way to civilian customers, others being destined for essential users. *Alan Earnshaw collection*

NOVEMBER 30, 1945

The Autocar

FOUNDED 1895   LARGEST CIRCULATION

6d

for the motorist whose car is always in use

The New HILLMAN MINX

THE HILLMAN MOTOR CAR CO. LTD., COVENTRY · A PRODUCT OF THE ROOTES GROUP

MOTOR · UNION INSURANCE CO. LTD.
ALL CLASSES OF INSURANCE TRANSACTED
10, ST. JAMES'S STREET, LONDON, S.W.1

The emotive scene as portrayed here is pure propaganda. The truth is that, in 1945, few cars were actually available as a result of limitations in production and shortages of raw materials. *Rootes publicity/*The Autocar

15

Right: More than 10,000 Phase I Minxes were supplied to essential users and military personnel up to 1942, which meant that, when production resumed post-war, much experience had been gained about the car's performance and reliability. *Rootes publicity/author's collection*

Left: An air of optimism is present in this 1947 advertising feature. Was life really as relaxed and affluent as this? One of the first specification changes to the post-war car was the adoption of Lockheed braking during 1947. *Rootes publicity/author's collection*

Below: The Phase II Minx was a restyled version of the pre-war monocoque Minx. Introduced late in 1947, the car served until an all-new Minx (Phase III) appeared the following year. *Rootes publicity/author's collection*

Rootes' London Service Station at Ladbroke Hall, Barlby Road, is pictured showing a huge consignment of Minxes along with Humber and other cars. *Rootes/Alan Earnshaw collection*

Though not immediately apparent, the Phase II Minx employed some technical modifications. The headlamps, smaller in diameter than before, made use of the latest 'pre-focus' technology (referred retrospectively to as 'semi-sealed' beams), with twin-filament bulbs for 'double-dipping' while sidelamps were provided by separate bulbs. When *The Motor* published its road test in December 1947, the car's lighting came in for some gentle criticism insomuch that, while there was an improvement to long distance illumination, there was less spread of light immediately in front of the vehicle.

Inside the car, front seats upholstered in a combination of cloth and leather had adjustment for rake, reach and, unusually for the period, height. A revised facia supported new style instruments so that the rectangular instruments, comprising a fuel gauge on one side and oil and ignition lights on the other, flanked a circular speedometer. Switches, too, were redesigned and there was space in which to fit the latest model HMV radio, which at the time was definitely a luxury accessory. With the adoption of 'synchromatic' column gear shift to supersede the floor change device, Rootes introduced some parity with the Humber Hawk. Despite Rootes' publicity material promising the column change to provide for exceptionally light finger-tip control, in practice it proved cumbersome with an annoying propensity to lock-up.

The Phase II Minx, despite being little more than a stopgap model while Rootes' engineers were employed developing an all-new model, was, in addition to the somewhat staid saloon, built as an estate car and as an attractive drophead coupé. Few of these derivatives were seen on British roads as most examples were exported. Carbodies, the highly reputable coachbuilding firm, constructed the dropheads by fabricating an entire body rearward of the scuttle (which was supplied by Rootes) complete with a three-position head. Once painted and trimmed, the vehicles were

17

despatched to Hillman for the fitting of mechanical components. Carbodies specialised in short production runs and, therefore, only a limited number of dropheads were actually produced.

It was not until the autumn of 1948 that Rootes was in a position to introduce an all-new Minx and, in common with a number of British manufacturers, adopted a style of body that was in keeping with the American idiom. This meant that the Minx and its contemporaries displayed a full-width frontal profile that merged wings with body, the latter being more commodious than previously as a result of being wider and having door panels extending over the running boards to form a flush side with front and rear wings.

The fact that the new Hillman, marketed as the Phase III Minx, demonstrated an American styling influence was entirely due to Rootes having consulted Raymond Loewy (1893-1986) on the design of the car. Loewy, an American who was born in Paris and who later achieved fame as a leading designer throughout the Art Deco era promoting so much fascination with streamlining, was responsible for a wealth of products from pencil sharpeners to refrigerators and steam locomotives. The factor that led Billy Rootes to consult Loewy was most likely the designer's work for Studebaker, which, in addition to influencing the Minx, was responsible for the emergence of the P4 Rover 75 at the 1949 London Motor Show.

When the new Minx was unveiled, Raymond Loewy's inspired design for Studebaker was indeed clearly evident, the design guru's influence extending beyond the Hillman marque to display a corporate Rootes' image. The design of the new Minx was sufficiently different to catch the attention of the leading motoring journals of the day and, in its motor show review edition, *The Motor* featured a cut-away drawing to illustrate the vehicle's importance.

Features about the new Minx that were considered novel included the full-width front bench seat, which, at a stretch, accommodated three people. The 'Opticurve' windscreen, whilst providing for good frontal visibility, added to the effect of roominess within the saloon. The driving position was comfortable and an attractive walnut veneer instrument panel added to the appeal of the car's interior appointment. Soft, yet supportive, suspension — independent front suspension appearing on the Minx for the first time — provided a pleasing ride quality and there was plentiful space within the cabin for small baggage. Particularly noteworthy was the capacious upward-opening boot with its separate compartment for the spare wheel and tools.

Not so favourable was the engine noise at medium speeds and, whilst no noisier than when fitted to previous cars, the 1,185cc side-valve engine appeared somewhat ancient compared to the many new overhead-valve designs coming onto the market.

Owing to the car's styling and construction rather than modifications made to the power train, the performance of the Phase III Minx was slightly more spirited than with previous models. Still, with maximum power of 35bhp at 4,100rpm, the new

Minx showed a top speed of 66mph, this being three miles per hour faster than the Phase II. Particularly impressive was the car's acceleration, 0-50mph reduced from 25.7 to 24.1 seconds. Fuel consumption, though, was slightly worse, the official figures showing the Phase III 1mpg average more than its predecessor.

The Phase III's relative lack of power was addressed within a few months of the car's introduction, which meant that the Hillman profited by having a larger engine in time for the 1949 London Motor Show. Reluctant to deviate from the side-valve

When it was introduced in September 1948, the Phase III Minx reflected a strong American influence. The car was designed in association with Raymond Loewy, the stylist who had been the inspiration behind Studebaker's cars. *Rootes publicity/author's collection*

From this delightful advertising piece it is hard to believe that Britain was severely affected by post-war austerity. For all its modernity, the Minx nevertheless relied on an ageing side-valve engine although it did feature independent front suspension and hydraulic brakes. *Rootes publicity/author's collection*

Rootes' marketing and advertising was always of good quality as depicted by this cameo publicising the new Minx.
Rootes publicity/author's collection

More substantial bumpers and sidelamps positioned beneath the headlamps identify this as a Phase IV model, which means that, out of sight, is a larger side-valve engine with a capacity of 1,265cc. *Rootes publicity/author's collection*

September 28, 1949.   The Motor

Showpiece

STAND 162
INTERNATIONAL MOTOR EXHIBITION
EARL'S COURT SEPT 28 - OCT 8

The HILLMAN
MINX MAGNIFICENT

Saloon · Convertible Coupe · Estate Car

There never was a car which made friends so quickly as the Minx. In use throughout the world, always the leader in its class, the Hillman Minx is roomy, comfortable, economical and thoroughly dependable. Big car comfort, independent front suspension, Synchromatic finger-tip gear control, Lockheed Hydraulic brakes, and the proved reliable Hillman Minx engine are features which are attracting a host of new friends in countries overseas, and which will ensure the lasting popularity of the Minx at home.

PRODUCTS OF THE ROOTES GROUP

LONDON SHOWROOMS & EXPORT DIVISION   ROOTES LTD   DEVONSHIRE HOUSE PICCADILLY LONDON W.1

THE **New** 21st ANNIVERSARY

Hillman Minx

SALOON
CALIFORNIA HARDTOP
CONVERTIBLE COUPE
ESTATE CAR

Completely new appearance
★
All round increased economy
★
More comfort
★
Still greater refinement in every detail

Yes, it really is 21 years since the Hillman Minx made its first popular appearance! A fine car even in 1932, the Minx has been progressively developed and improved ever since; and today, with well over 21,000 million miles of happy family motoring to its credit, the Minx is part of the fabric of life in almost every country in the world. To celebrate this great occasion, here is the 21st Anniversary Minx ... the most brilliant, the thriftiest, the most reliable family car of all time!

21 years and
21,000 MILLION MILES have perfected this car for you!

★ PRODUCT OF THE ROOTES GROUP ★

For the new Minx, Hillman resurrected the Magnificent name. By showing an attractive young lady at the wheel, Rootes cleverly appealed to a wide and affluent market. *Rootes publicity/author's collection*

A redesigned Minx was launched to coincide with the 21st anniversary of the Hillman Minx. This was the Mk VI complete with subtle restyling that included a modified radiator grille. *Rootes publicity/author's collection*

Top: Post-war, Hillmans were never far from the sporting scene. The Minx was to be found entering the Monte Carlo Rally in 1950, the year the car pictured was registered, with eight cars, a similar number being entered in 1951. *H. B. Clayton/Author's collection*

Above Left: A popular version of the Minx was the drophead, the car pictured here being a Phase IV. Carbodies built the early convertibles, Thrupp & Maberly the later models. *Rootes publicity/Alan Earnshaw collection*

Above: This Phase III Minx competed in the 1949 Monte Carlo Rally, having been despatched from Glasgow. Pictured with the car are driver Hiskins and his crew. The car finished 70th out of 135 finishers; another Minx, driven by Harper, Evan and Cook, finished 15th. *Rootes publicity/Alan Earnshaw collection*

layout, Rootes' engineers squeezed a further 80cc from the ageing unit that had been introduced in the early 1930s. The power increase was sufficient to summon a Phase IV designation, the car's maximum speed rising by one mile per hour to 67mph but advantageous effects of the engine re-design were its smooth running and typical 32mpg fuel consumption. It was the detail changes to the engine design that were most important, such as the counter-balanced three-bearing crankshaft and the water pump bolted to the front of the cylinder block that aimed coolant more directly onto the exhaust valve seatings. Essential to the smoother operation of the car was the employment of improved flexible rubber engine mountings.

A bigger and better **Hillman** range!

The Hillman Californian. Looked at, or looked out of, the view is superb. Windows drop down clear into the body panels, and up or down, for all-round vision the sky's the limit. Dual colour schemes.

The Hillman Minx Convertible. Triple success—as an open car with fold-away hood, a town coupé, or the comfort of a saloon. Three cars in one, to match any mood, any occasion, any weather.

This motoring year, looks make news! The 'Big Car' beauty of the new Minx Saloon, with added luggage space to match its five-seater comfort . . . The exciting international elegance of the Hillman Californian, style-setter for years to come . . . The sleek grace of the Minx Convertible, weatherwise in its easy adaptability to every occasion . . . The all-purpose smartness and style of the Estate Car, equally at home in town or country.

Yes, looks make news. But the best news of all—the choice is yours. See them at the Motor Show. Then try them on the road at your Hillman dealers, and you'll agree: no car more surely earned its world-wide fame. It's big car motoring at light car cost at Hillman's incomparable best.

EARLS COURT **stand 136**

Rootes Group Cars
make a wonderful show

HUMBER   HILLMAN   SUNBEAM - TALBOT

The Hillman Estate Car. Room to move — fast. Here's strength for the all-purpose, all-weather work on the estate, style and comfort for touring or town. Wide rear doors for easy loading and a fold-flat rear seat for added space.

Appearing at the same time as the 21st Anniversary edition of the Minx was the Californian, a car that had much appeal. The latter, in reality, was a hardtop version of the convertible, which is also featured here. *Rootes publicity/author's collection*

Eight months separated the Mk VI and VII Minxes, the latter having a larger rear window, greater capacity boot along with detail changes to the facia and instrumentation. *Rootes publicity Alan Earnshaw collection*

For the 1950 model year the Minx's image was boosted by the introduction of a number of relatively minor modifications, such as the provision of separate sidelamps positioned beneath the headlamps and the fitting of extended and reshaped bumpers that gave the car a more substantial profile.

When the Phase V Minx made its debut in the autumn of 1951 few technical and styling changes were evident. The new model designation was apparently little more than a prompt to those motorists anxious to own the latest car. The subtle external differences between this and the Phase IV amounted to additional chrome on the grille, front wings, front doors and leading edges of the rear wings.

Appearing nearly 18 months after the Phase V in early 1953, it was the Mk VI — Rootes had dropped the 'Phase' designation in favour of 'Mark' — that caused the most interest by virtue of a restyled radiator grille along with a lower bonnet line which gave the Minx a new identity. The design changes coincided with the Minx's 21st anniversary and were not confined to the car's frontal styling. Wrap-around bumpers afforded additional protection to the most vulnerable parts of the vehicle while faired-in rear lamps marked the extremities of the body, the overall length of the vehicle having been increased by two inches. For driver and passenger comfort the heating and ventilation system was improved by provision of a fresh-air intake positioned on the right hand side of the radiator grille. The facia too was new, as was the redesigned steering wheel.

By far the most dramatic event of the Minx's 21st anniversary celebration was the introduction of the Californian Coupé, with its attractive closed four-seater coachwork. Instead of being constructed by Carbodies, the Californian, and indeed all convertibles and estates after the Mk V of 1953, were built in-house by Thrupp & Maberly. Being priced the same as the convertible, the Californian sported a wrap-around rear window and radially-opening rear quarterlights. The car's light interior and luxury appointment were, as its name suggests, designed primarily for the export market, America in particular, though it was also popular with British motorists. Features of the Californian included its excellent all-round visibility, luxury fittings that included a radio and a clock, white wall tyres, 70mph performance and, with the need to stow the hood, enhanced boot capacity.

The Californian epitomised Britain's emergence from post-war austerity as well as reflecting a distinct American ideology in respect of motor design. The car displayed a number of luxury features including a split-bench front seat, radially-opening quarter lights and a wrap-around rear window. *Alan Earnshaw*

The Minx attracted a diverse clientele, such was the car's reputation for quality, reliability and affordability. The car pictured is clearly revered by its lady owner. *Author's collection*

The under bonnet of this 1954 Minx is the subject of much interest and justifiably so, as this Mk VIII is fitted with the new 1,390cc ohv engine. Introduced for 1955, only the de Luxe Minx, along with the Drophead and Californian, were fitted with the more powerful engine, standard editions and estate cars having side-valve units. *Rootes publicity/Alan Earnshaw collection*

Raymond Loewy's influence remained evident in later Minxes, the car illustrated being a Series I convertible. This emotive piece of advertising portrays an idyllic and carefree scene that belies the fact that drophead models were selling in fewer numbers than might have been anticipated. This was a malaise common to other car makers of the period. *Author's collection*

Within months of the introduction of the Series I Minx saloon, an estate version was unveiled. Novel features were the split tailgate and divided rear seats, which could be folded flat in order to provide additional carrying space. The image depicts a later version dating from the late 1950s or early 1960s. *Rootes publicity/author's collection*

An entirely new Minx was unveiled in the spring of 1956 and, to emphasise the model's importance, it was designated the Series I Minx. The Loewy influence was still very evident. Smiles all round, for the new Minx engendered huge demand that kept Ryton running at full capacity. *Rootes publicity/Alan Earnshaw collection*

Rootes celebrated 25 years of Minx production by launching the Jubilee model to coincide with the introduction of the Series II Minx. Pictured against a majestic backdrop, the Jubilee Minx's two-tone paintwork and white wall tyres are seen to good effect. In the background can be seen the convertible version. *Rootes publicity/author's collection*

Later in 1953 the Mk VI gave way to the Mk VII, which was given a larger rear window and an extended boot, the interior of which was illuminated by the rear lights. A major development came in the autumn of 1954 when an optional overhead-valve engine of 1,390cc was offered to result in the Mk VIII designation. The new engine was fitted to the saloon, now known as the Minx de Luxe, and the Californian, though the side-valve engine remained available on what was referred to as the Minx Special, a basic, thus cheaper, saloon, the estate car and Husky. The latter is discussed in a later chapter.

In conjunction with the increase in power, the Minx's axle ratio was altered from 5.22:1 to 4.778:1 in order to provide for a livelier performance compared to the side-valve engined car. Cruising speed was an easy 65mph and the top speed was nearly 10mph faster, such performance leading to the respectable average fuel consumption of 35mpg. Another advantage was quicker acceleration through the gears, which, combined with the car's improved performance, called for wider section tyres to be specified and the removal of the anti-roll torsion bar from the rear axle to the front suspension. In order that the ohv-engined car could be easily identified from its siblings, the radiator grille was modified to incorporate a horizontal bar at the mid-point.

Car showrooms of the mid-1950s had little glamour. This Jubilee Minx, offered for sale by Rootes' agent Thomas Head, is pictured in what can only be described as stark surroundings. *Author's collection*

By the mid-1950s the degree of styling evolution in respect of British and European cars meant that the Minx had become firmly entrenched in a past era. The shape of the new generation Minx, which was launched in the spring of 1956, was actually revealed several months earlier at the time of the London Motor Show, under the guise of the rakish new Sunbeam Rapier. The treatment given to the first Rootes-built Sunbeam, albeit the car was constructed as a two-door coupé, was, therefore, something of a test-bed for the Minx.

In similar fashion to its predecessor, the new Hillman, now referred to as the Series I Minx, was again styled under the influence of Raymond Loewy's studio and mirrored work undertaken for Studebaker. Compare what was happening on the Studebaker front with such models as the Regal and President, and the family connection becomes obvious. With its sleek profile, ample glass area that included a large wrap-around rear window, prominent front wings, the line of which neatly extended to the tail, the new Minx demonstrated just how modern, roomy and comfortable this affordable mid-size family vehicle was. The front of the Minx looked as striking as the rest of car with its high-set headlamps, gently sloping bonnet and full-width air intake.

Additional to substantial restyling, Rootes engineers beefed up the ohv engine that had been introduced only a few months earlier. By raising the compression ratio from 7:1 to 8:1 to provide a further 8bhp, the top speed of the Series I Minx was in excess of 80mph. All this was achieved without seriously compromising fuel

This Series III convertible has been the subject of a complete restoration on behalf of its owner, Reg Barker, who is at the wheel. These cars were often finished in pastel colours and are now eagerly sought by enthusiasts. *Author*

Instrumentation fitted to the convertible and de Luxe models was comprehensive, a feature lacking on many mid-price cars of the period. *Author*

economy, *The Motor* road test revealing 30mpg averaged over 1,162 miles taking in a variety of terrain and driving conditions.

The interior appointment of the Series I Minx was as modern looking as its exterior styling. A welcome feature was the improvement in the amount of passenger space compared to previous models. This was realised by redesigning the chassis so that the engine and gearbox were moved forwards over the front suspension, and positioning the rear axle farther rearward. Owing to an increase in wheelbase length, entry and exit to the passenger cabin was made all the easier; moreover, the continuing adoption of column gear change accentuated the front compartment's roominess. Instrumentation was centrally located and stylishly American, there being provision for a clock and radio, both of which were optional extras.

A drophead version of the new Series I was also available. Hillman's new open tourer proved to be an attractively packaged car, especially as its dual-tone colour scheme and double swage line give it a sporting air. With a price premium of around £100 over that of the saloon, the convertible attracted a select clientele and, therefore, demand was limited. The convertible, which could be specified with Alexander Engineering tuning modifications, remained in the Hillman catalogue until the summer of 1962.

There was no shortage of customers eager to buy the new-look Minx that went on sale at a shade under £774 inclusive of purchase tax. Although there was little difficulty in selling the Minx, Rootes, when introducing modifications to the design of the car, however seemingly insignificant these might have seemed, changed the model appellation to Series II only 15 months later, presumably to help stimulate sales.

In the company of a Wolseley and a Mini, this Series III Minx served as a training vehicle with the Metropolitan Police and is pictured at the Hendon skid pan. *Metropolitan Police*

Predating the Series II by two months, Hillman launched its all-new five-door Minx estate car. This was a compact, yet eminently useful, vehicle that adopted the lines of the ubiquitous American station wagon and featured a split tailgate and flat loading platform when the rear seats were folded. As a small to medium size estate car, the Minx estate was a strong seller until 1962 when it was replaced by the Super Minx estate car.

The Series II was launched to coincide with the 25th anniversary of the Hillman Minx and it was known as the Jubilee edition. Several design features were evident, including a restyled grille and bumpers. The latter modification was designed to meet the rough treatment faced by cars exported to certain countries. Mechanical changes involved lightening the steering gear to improve low-speed manoeuvring, as well as modifications to the camshaft that had the effect of increasing torque at low engine speeds without raising the maximum power output. For the first time, the Minx could be specified with Lockheed's semi-automatic Manumatic transmission to facilitate effortless gear changing via the column-mounted selector and centrifugal clutch.

By resurrecting the Special Saloon concept, a lead-in economy model was added to the Series II catalogue. Featuring separate front seats and a floor-mounted centrally-positioned gear lever, this simply attired Minx was characterised by its single body colour, plastic leathercloth upholstery, rubber matting, and simplified instrument console. Slightly smaller section tyres (5.00x15 compared to 5.60x15) were specified. The resulting differences in handling were applauded by some motoring commentators.

A larger engine, a new front grille and revised body trim mouldings heralded the Series III Minx for 1959. Utilising the 1,494cc engine, used in the Singer Gazelle and Sunbeam Rapier, was a step towards rationalising power units throughout the Rootes' catalogue, though the Minx's maximum power output was some 7.5bhp lower. Raising the compression ratio slightly to improve medium speed torque and re-gearing the final drive to obtain a five per cent reduction in engine revs, led to improved acceleration.

The tail fins identify this as a series IIIA Minx, in this instance with duo-tone paint and white wall tyres. Series III cars, introduced in September 1958, had engines enlarged to 1,494cc and, a year later, when the IIIA appeared, there was the option of Smiths' Easidrive semi-automatic transmission and a floor-mounted gear change as standard. *Rootes publicity/Alan Earnshaw collection*

The revised radiator grille gave the car a more modern appearance. Column shift was retained on the de Luxe model, as was the centrally positioned instrument console. Within a year of its introduction, the Series III was superseded by the IIIA, which sported even more power, modified rear wings with rolled-over fins and yet another revision to the radiator grille. Finally, the column gear change gear was abandoned in favour of floor change. For motorists wanting fully automatic transmission, Smiths' Easidrive replaced Lockheed's Manumatic arrangement. Less than a year later, Rootes specified for the Minx a hypoid-bevel rear axle in place of the time honoured spiral affair, this being sufficient to summon the IIIB appellation.

The Hillman Minx, as typified by this late Series III example, was a favourite with British motorists who probably had little knowledge the car had been influenced by Raymond Loewy's design for the American Studebaker. *Author*

Above Left and Right: Pictured is a Series IIIA/B, which had a 1,494cc engine to give a 78mph top speed. Though by now a floor-mounted gear change had replaced the column type, the handbrake remained to the right of the driver's seat on right-hand drive cars. *Andrew Minney*

Announced in the autumn of 1961, the Series IIIC Minx received a larger engine, the 1,592cc unit providing a maximum output of 52.8bhp at 4,100rpm. Only minor styling changes were evident, the most apparent being a single swage line moulding, full height tail lights and Minx script added to the boot lid. Since its inception the Minx had always received excellent reviews but, by 1962, road test reports were becoming increasingly critical of the model's bench front seat and its lack of adjustment. While straight line performance was on a par with more modern vehicles, handling and ride qualities were also beginning to show their age.

The Series IIIC Minx remained in production until 1963, by which time Rootes, having rationalised the Minx range by dropping the basic Special Saloon, decided to give its bread-and-butter model, now known as the Minx 1600, a serious makeover. Rather than give it a Series IV nomenclature, which had originally been chosen for the Super Minx, the Series IIIC's successor attracted the Series V designation. During 1963 a little milestone was reached on the other side of the world when Isuzu Motors of Japan, who built the Hillman Minx under licence, produced the 50,000th example of the car at its Fujisawa factory.

Immediately obvious about the Series V's profile were its lower bonnet, revised radiator grille and bumpers fitted with rubber-faced overriders. Other revisions included a flat roof, larger doors, rear quarters that dispensed with the wrap-around design, a simple but wide rear screen and angular rear wings minus fins. New door handles and wheel trims, a straight-through swage line and 13in wheels completed the restyling.

Inside the car the modern facia with instruments ahead of the driver and small controls centrally placed was favourably received. The appointment of the cabin meant that separate front seats provided optimum comfort, the driver's seat rising in height as

When the IIIC Minx was introduced in 1961, it featured an engine increased in capacity to 1,592cc. Testing cars on foreign roads was a matter of great importance at Rootes and one in which Billy Rootes took much interest, often joining the test teams to see for himself how the cars performed. *Rootes publicity/Alan Earnshaw collection*

it moved forward. The handbrake lever remained to the driver's right on right-hand drive editions. On cars specified with automatic transmission, Borg Warner's type 35 gearbox replaced Smiths' Easidrive system. Minxes with automatic transmission, together with cars destined for export to America, were fitted with the Super Minx engine, which developed 6bhp more power. Other mechanical improvements included adoption of front-wheel disc brakes, larger fuel tank and elimination of chassis grease points.

This is the face of the Minx between 1956 and 1963, a period when engines were given more power and transmissions were modified to provide floor change gear shifts along with the option of semi-automatic gearboxes. Series III cars from the IIIA of 1959 had rear wing tailfins, a feature that disappeared with introduction of the restyled Series V in 1963. *Author*

For customers requiring greater levels of performance than would normally be available, Rootes offered the Alexander Minx with its 92mph top speed and upper 80s cruising potential. Compared to the standard model 1600 Minx, which took 37.5 seconds to reach 70mph from rest, the Alexander version took a mere 21.8 seconds. Alexander Engineering had a long history of tuning Hillmans and, in respect of the Series V Minx, this amounted to raising the power output from 52.8bhp at 4,100rpm to 78bhp at 4,900rpm. To achieve this level of performance twin 1.5in SU carburettors were fitted to a polished alloy induction manifold with polished and matched ports; combustion chambers were reshaped and the compression ratio raised from 8.3 to 8.6:1. Braking was modified by the fitting of a Lockheed vacuum servo unit to lighten the pedal load and provide for a more sensitive feel to the system. Inside the car, a wood-rimmed steering wheel was fitted, along with a rev-counter fitted to the right hand side of the facia. Apart from trim detail, which included dedicated badging and the addition of simulated alloy rear quarter panels, the only other significant modification was to move the battery from under the bonnet to the boot.

The Series V stayed into production until the autumn of 1965, after which Rootes announced the Series VI, which was to be the last of the traditional Minx models. Fitted with the Rootes-designed 1,725cc five-bearing long-stroke engine, which gave the car exceptionally smooth performance and synchromesh on first gear, the only distinguishing features between this and the Series V were its revised interior trim with heat-welded plastic upholstery, a restyled facia incorporating a rectangular instrument console and dedicated '1725' badging fitted to the lower rear of each front wing.

The family favourite Minx was dropped from Rootes' catalogue in the spring of 1967. Replacing it was a new generation Minx — the body shape of which was shared with other models in the Rootes' range — the Hillman Hunter, the Singer Gazelle and the Vogue along with the Humber Sceptre. Of the new look 'Arrow' Minx, *Motor* in its 1967 road test described the car — arguably condescendingly — as being 'one of those sound, unexciting family cars that does most things well and nothing particularly badly'.

The Series V Minx, seen at Ryton, was introduced in the autumn of 1963 and featured front-wheel disc brakes, optional Borg Warner automatic transmission and, from 1964, an all-synchromesh gearbox. Interiors were updated to include a new style facia and instrumentation. *Rootes publicity/Alan Earnshaw collection*

The Super Minx

MOTOR industry commentators had little difficulty in seeing that, by the 1960s, the Hillman Minx was beginning to show its age. Despite its rugged and reliable engineering, the products of rival car-makers were not only looking more modern, they were also demonstrating levels of performance with which the Minx could not easily compete. Moreover, the Minx had acquired a label as being utterly conservative to the point that it was unexciting; a dubious attribute, perhaps, but one that appealed to a particular type of motorist who would not have dared sample front-wheel drive nor, for that matter, would they have considered purchasing a foreign car.

The answer to Hillman's predicament was to launch a new range of cars encompassing up-to-the-minute styling and technical features that would attract a wider clientele. But herein lay the problem: the model that was to replace the Minx grew to such an extent that it emerged substantially bigger than had been planned. Billy and Reginald Rootes, being reluctant to let the traditional Minx fade into obscurity, decreed that the Minx be retained as well as introducing the new, and larger, model. Despite the temptation of the design team to inject some innovation into the new car, management was opposed again to producing anything that might be viewed as anything other than safely cautious and completely conventional.

The dilemma within the company was deeper than merely a whim to preserve the traditional image and to keep the ageing Minx in production. Not only was it considered that a new car would be expensive to develop, profitability could well be compromised by offering too many models, especially as the Singer Gazelle was, in effect, little more than a refined and better attired Minx. There were also the Sunbeam and Humber marques to consider; the former appealed to the sporting motorist and was far removed from the traditional Hillman customer, whilst the latter was pitched firmly in the luxury sector. Nevertheless, the body styling employed for the Super Minx and Singer Vogue was later to be shared with the Sceptre, Humber's new compact saloon.

Above Right: Rootes had intended to introduce an entirely new styling theme for what was to be the Series IV Minx. Several ideas were proposed by senior stylist Ted White, this mock-up showing just one of the many ideas that culminated in the Super Minx of autumn 1961. *Rootes publicity/Alan Earnshaw collection*

Note the styling differences between the Super Minx and the prototype shown in the photograph above. The positioning of the sidelamps was considered novel at the time of the car's introduction, while overall the Super Minx provided for greater comfort and more spacious accommodation than the Minx. *Rootes publicity*

The period in which the new catalogue of cars was developed also proved to be a difficult time for Rootes; not only had the decision been taken to build the Imp, which would be a costly project to put into production, a disastrous strike that shattered the firm's finances had erupted at the company's body pressing factory in West London. To compound matters, a slump in British car sales in the early 1960s, a malaise that affected other manufacturers (particularly BMC), hit Rootes badly.

The styling and design of the new and larger Minx were undertaken by Humber under the guidance of Ted White, all links with the Loewy studio having by this time been severed. Ted White's stylish offering with sidelamps sandwiched between the headlamps and wing crown, the deeply curved windscreen with thin roof pillars, wrap-around rear window and finned rear wings, was designed to compete head-on with designs emanating from Dagenham and Luton whilst being more conventional than those which Issigonis was devising for BMC.

Even if the Super Minx was lavishly sculptured compared to the shape of the existing Minx, its technical specification was anything but inventive, Rootes' philosophy being that its customers wanted nothing to do with radical innovation. Compared to its sister car, the Super Minx sported a spacious and well appointed interior, the optional separate front seats offering more comfort and support than the standard bench. Wide doors made for easy entrance and exit and, once inside, the driver discovered an attractively-styled facia with circular instruments alongside controls that were conveniently placed. In traditional Hillman manner, the parking brake on right-hand drive cars was still located to the driver's right.

The wrap-around styling feature is seen to good effect on this left-hand drive Super Minx. Interior accommodation comprised a front bench seat as standard, bucket seats being optional. From the outset the car had drum brakes but, in 1962, the Series II car had disc brakes and optional Borg Warner automatic transmission. *Author*

Whilst this mock-up wears Sunbeam Rapier IV nomenclature, the image demonstrates how the design for the Hillman Super Minx was utilised for other Rootes' products: the Singer Vogue and Humber Sceptre. *Rootes publicity/Alan Earnshaw collection*

Introduced in the autumn of 1961, the Super Minx was powered by Hillman's 62bhp 1,592cc four-cylinder engine that was to become standard across the Minx range of cars. In essence, the car developed degrees of power, performance and handling that were, as suggested within the road test published by *The Motor*, 'somewhat unexciting'. It was, though, an extremely forgiving car when it came to maintenance, all under-bonnet components being easily accessible. Whilst the car was fitted with manual transmission as standard, specification of Smiths' Easidrive automatic transmission was optional. Few cars were supplied with this gearbox as, within a year, the Borg Warner type automatic gearbox was specified to coincide with the announcement of the Mk II Super Minx.

Modifications that brought about the Mk II model designation included upgrading the braking system. Front disc brakes were fitted, drums being retained at the rear, the combination resulting in impressive stopping power. The car's interior was also upgraded, separate front seats becoming a standard feature.

The Super Minx Convertible made its debut in the summer of 1962 and incorporated modifications that were to feature a couple of months later on the saloon. Making available a drophead derivative of the Super Minx was an important development as too few quantity produced European cars were offered with the alternative of a convertible body style. The finish of the car and the equipment offered as standard were seen as being superior to similar vehicles, especially as the hood was weatherproof, draught free and easy to operate. Despite being

The Super Minx showed none of the Raymond Loewy influence that had inspired the post-war Minxes. Engine and transmission for the car was borrowed from the Minx, though front suspension was modified. *Rootes publicity/Alan Earnshaw collection*

The Super Minx was offered as a drophead coupé from mid-1962. Thrupp & Maberly were responsible for building the car, which remained in production for two years after which it was discontinued. *Rootes publicity/author's collection*

An estate car version of the Super Minx was introduced at the same time as the convertible. Production was undertaken by Rootes rather than Thrupp & Maberly as the coachbuilder did not have the capacity to build them. *Rootes publicity/Alan Earnshaw collection*

Customers buying a Super Minx estate car or similar Rootes model discovered the split tailgate to be extremely useful, as there was no need to drop the lower section when loading small items into the back of the car. *Rootes publicity/Alan Earnshaw collection*

This picture of a Super Minx estate car illustrates the capacity that the model afforded. When transporting large and bulky items the rear seats folded down to allow for a flat load platform. *Rootes publicity/Alan Earnshaw collection*

heavier than the saloon by 1cwt, as a result of the weight of the hood and the necessary chassis strengthening, performance of the Convertible was only slightly compromised compared to that of the saloon. The car's 70mph cruising speed, whilst barely breathtaking, was sufficient for most customers, any criticism being mainly restricted to gear ratio spacing, which meant holding on to third gear when attempting to take twisting routes with verve.

At the same time as the Convertible, which was priced at around £100 more than the saloon, was introduced, Rootes announced an estate car derivative of the Super Minx. With its capacious interior, which afforded ample load space, the model's popularity was assured from the very beginning, particularly as Rootes had originally ruled that there would not be estate variants of the Singer Vogue or Humber Sceptre. Ultimately the former was offered as an estate car but was only built in limited numbers. Technically, the Super Minx estate cars were identical to the saloons, save for relatively minor modifications to trim and suspension settings.

Both convertible and estate Super Minx derivatives were constructed by Thrupp & Maberly, the convertible featuring the coachbuilder's two-position head in deference to Carbodies' trademark three-position design. Thrupp & Maberly understandably undertook most of Rootes' bespoke coachwork, though Carbodies were responsible for the Singer Vogue Estate simply because there was insufficient capacity at Thrupp & Maberly. Too few customers, it seemed, wanted the thrill and enjoyment that a drophead coupé promised and, in the summer of 1964, the model disappeared from the catalogue.

Three years after its launch, the Super Minx III was introduced complete with restyling. This publicity image shows that the wrap-around treatment was abandoned in favour of a flatter roof and revised rear profile.
Rootes publicity/Alan Earnshaw collection

Coinciding with the drophead's demise, the Mk II Super Minx saloon was discontinued in favour of the Mk III. The new model was given a styling facelift, which, though perceived as being more modern and thus competing with similarly-sized cars from Ford, Vauxhall and BMC, arguably detracted from its predecessor's attractive appearance. Immediately noticeable were the flatter roofline, modified rear pillars and an almost flat rear screen, all of which gave rise to the abandonment of the wrap-around styling. The re-sculpturing of the cabin allowed for improved interior accommodation; not only did front seat passengers enjoy the luxury of fully reclining seats, rear seat passengers were afforded increased space while larger doors facilitated easier entry and exit. Mechanically, an all-synchromesh gearbox improved the car's driving characteristics.

In its modified shape the Super Minx remained available for no more than a year before being fitted with the Rootes' five-bearing 1,725cc engine in mid-1965. Enlargement of the faithful four-cylinder engine was made possible by lengthening the stroke by 6.35mm, thus making it undersquare. There were limitations in achieving the longer stroke simply because the cylinder block could not be deepened, and, to accommodate the modification, the connecting rods were shortened.

Engine development, along with a requirement by the company's engineering division to reduce weight, had been conducted over a long period. The original design had a normal cylinder block wall thickness of 0.31in, but this was progressively reduced to 0.25in, 0.19in and finally to 0.15in, the latter being specified for the 1,725cc unit. With such reduced casting thickness, there existed a problem with vibration and noise transmission, the remedy being to convert the cylinder block to accommodate a five-bearing crankshaft. The transition to five bearings was a relatively simple process though major alterations to the crankcase were necessary.

Owing to the greater rigidity that five bearings afforded, Rootes, for the first time, specified a crank cast from spheroidal graphite iron. Bearing materials compatible with the cast-iron crank were chosen, these being white metal for the main bearings and aluminium-tin for the big-ends. The increased engine capacity also called for a modified air cleaner and the fitting of a Zenith 34 IV carburettor, the latter enhancing overall performance. Apart from the aforementioned components, most engine parts remained interchangeable with those of the superseded 1,592cc unit.

Only the most minor styling changes were evident, these included a modified combined indicator and sidelamp unit with an amber insert to meet changing regulations, a new plinth mounting for the rear number plate and the addition of a security device on the quarterlight windows fitted to the front doors. Though there was no change to the facia design and layout, the comprehensive instrumentation was restyled and made easier to read with improved vertical calibrations.

When fitted to the Super Minx, the 1,725cc engine produced only 65bhp at 4,800rpm and was, therefore, lightly stressed considering the output was increased to 92.5bhp when fitted to the Sunbeam Alpine. Laycock overdrive was optional on the Super Minx and facilitated sustained speeds of 85-90mph without causing engine stress or excessive oil consumption. Average fuel consumption of 20.8mpg was considered to be relatively poor when the Super Minx was subjected to media road testing, the figure falling short by comparison with other cars of similar size and power. Not all owners drove their cars as aggressively as test drivers and, under normal circumstances, around 30mpg was achievable. In acceleration the Hillman took less than 18 seconds to reach 60mph from a standing start, an enviable level of performance compared to what the majority of medium sized cars could then achieve.

In terms of handling, the 1,725cc Super Minx attracted some criticism in respect of its heavy steering when parking. In all other respects it proved to be highly commendable, particularly the efficiency of the braking system that operated without the need of servo assistance.

The Super Minx saloon remained in production until 1966, the car being discontinued immediately prior to the introduction of the Rex Fleming-styled Hillman Hunter. Super Minx estates stayed in production longer and disappeared from the catalogue early in 1967.

Below & Bottom Right: The Super Minx would have replaced the Minx had it not been for continuing development that produced a car that was substantially bigger than intended. Billy Rootes was loath to see the traditional Minx disappear and, therefore, the Super Minx became additional in the Hillman catalogue. The original Super Minx of 1961 featured 'wrap-around' rear styling until 1964 when the car, as shown here, underwent significant restyling of the rear quarters. The estate cars were popular as they had an enormous carrying capacity. *Rootes publicity/Author's collection/Author*

A late Super Minx pictured near Stirling in Scotland. From 1965 the Super Minx range was updated with the 1,725cc engine and, in 1966, the Hillman Hunter replaced the saloon. Super Minx estate cars remained in production until 1967. *Author*

Hillman Husky

THE Hillman Husky, owing to its size, styling and functional design, quickly acquired a popular following after its introduction at the 1954 London Motor Show. Although smaller than the Minx, the size of the Husky was not perceived as being a disadvantage, particularly as the vehicle was seen to have an excellent carrying capacity. Though having only two doors whereas the Minx had four, access to the Husky's interior was not in any way impaired, especially as the car featured wide door apertures and the provision of a full height and width side-hinged tailgate. At the time of its introduction the small Hillman was viewed as being a utility vehicle by virtue of its van-shape profile; indeed the Husky's body structure was shared with the Commer Cob. In retrospect, judging by the design of cars that were to evolve decades later, the Husky clearly predicted a popular styling influence.

The choice of Husky as a model name for this functional Hillman proved popular within the motor trade, the car successfully serving countless families with its versatile and reliable qualities at a time when the market for estate cars had yet to flourish. The design of the vehicle had, nevertheless, overtones of the immediate post-war

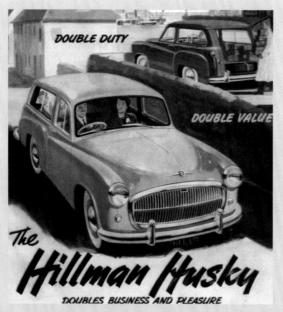

DOUBLE DUTY

DOUBLE VALUE

The **Hillman Husky**

DOUBLES BUSINESS AND PLEASURE

Left: The Hillman Husky was based on the Hillman Minx estate car but designed with a shorter wheelbase. When the Minx was upgraded with an overhead-valve engine, the Husky soldiered on using the long-serving side-valve affair. With its side-hinged tailgate and folding rear seats to afford a large carrying space, the Husky served as what might be termed a multi-purpose vehicle and, as such, offered functional yet comfortable motoring. *Rootes publicity/author's collection*

Opposite: Designed as being a practical three-door estate car, the Husky featured a full-width and height side-opening tailgate. Rear seats, when not in use, folded flat to allow for ample carrying space, the spare wheel being located beneath the luggage floor. Husky marketing was aimed at young families wanting an inexpensive but practical runabout that promised reliable and affordable motoring. *Rootes publicity/Author's collection*

The Husky was planned to be a compact all-purpose vehicle. It was derived from the Minx, although 14in shorter in length, and sported a frontal styling similar to its larger sibling. *Rootes publicity/Alan Earnshaw collection*

years when vans were converted to practical estate type cars by a number of specialist converters such as Martin Walter Ltd and Harold Radford. Such conversions were ideal for motorists with growing families or traders running small businesses at a time when new vehicles were largely unavailable to the home market owing to Britain's export drive, in addition to limitations in production and supply of raw materials.

'A compact and economy vehicle which plays many roles with efficiency and charm' is how *The Motor* described the Husky late in 1954, the model having been first shown at the London Motor Show at Earl's Court a month or so before.

The styling of the Husky was very much akin to the Minx, though in size the former was scaled-down so as to be 14in shorter but only a quarter of an inch narrower than its sibling. The frontal aspect of both cars was so similar to make evident a near identical design, the only minor departures being the badging, sidelamps and trim detail.

The utility characteristic of the Husky gave the car its welcome versatility, the rear seat being easily folded to allow a flat loading space aft of the separate front seats. This was an ideal situation for motorists wanting to make the most of the car's interior space, especially at holiday time or when the need arose to transport large and bulky items. Likewise, the Husky particularly suited business users who were able to use the vehicle for commercial purposes during the week and as a commodious family runabout at weekends and holidays.

The Husky competed with the Morris Minor Traveller de Luxe in terms of size, performance and fuel consumption. Compared to the 803cc four-cylinder Morris, the 1,265cc Hillman appeared to be amply powered, though maximum speeds of both cars were within 1mph of each other, this despite the Morris's unladen kerb weight of 16½cwt, which was 1½cwt lighter than its rival. Price-wise, the Husky at £564 19s 2d had the advantage over the BMC car by some £57, a significant amount of money in 1955.

The Husky helped set a trend, its contemporaries including utility or estate versions of some of Britain's favourite cars. These included the Standard Ten hp

This emotive publicity photograph depicts a family's overland trek from England to the Antipodes, the Husky in question arriving in South Australia in excellent condition. Sadly there is no indication as to the identity of the family concerned nor the location of the Rootes garage. *Rootes publicity/Alan Earnshaw collection*

Companion estate car, Ford's Anglia and Prefect in the guise of the Escort and Squire, and the Countryman editions of the Austin A30 and A35. Foreign cars, too, followed the vogue in the form of Fiat's innovative 600 Multipla and Renault's Juvaquatre, the latter displaying its pre-war origins.

Instead of the Husky receiving the Hillman Minx's newly introduced 1,390cc ohv engine, it was fitted with the side-valve unit. Despite the engine configuration, the Husky proved to be a sprightly performer compared to the side-valve Minx, typical fuel consumption averaging 33-35mpg compared to its big brother's 29mpg. The top speeds of both cars were comparable, the Husky mustering a fraction under 68mph, only 1mph slower than the Minx, albeit the car's 'comfortable' cruising speed was around 50mph. These figures are academic and should be viewed in the context that the Husky was tuned for economy to develop 35bhp at 4,100rpm whereas the Minx's maximum power peaked at 37.5bhp at 4,200rpm. Relative to this are the Husky's altered axle ratio and use of smaller tyres to provide slightly lower gearing.

In designing the Husky, Hillman engineers chose to abandon the Minx's column gear shift in favour of a central floor change. Similar to the Minx, the Husky's instrumentation was centrally located within the facia, the design of the binnacle being less elaborate than that seen on the more expensive car. The suspension, too, was forgiving bearing in mind it was required to cope with a wide margin between minimum and maximum loads in relation to the vehicle's unladen weight. Being a utility vehicle, noise levels were more noticeable than would be the case with the Minx, and the seating remained supportive and comfortable despite reduced cushion thickness and restricted driver's seat adjustment.

Fewer than 42,000 Huskies were built before a revised model was introduced in January 1958. Oddly marketed as the Series 1, the new Husky featured a similar three-door body arrangement to its predecessor. Though built on a short-wheelbase version of the Minx estate car, the wheelbase on the new model was two inches longer than that of the original vehicle. The length of the car being 3½in greater overall, customers were quick to appreciate the extra roominess and load capacity. The side-valve engine was at last consigned to history and the specifying of the 1,390cc ohv unit provided for improved performance.

Apart from the drive train, the most fundamental aspect about the new model was the all-new bodywork. Immediately evident were the bonnet arrangement and radiator design, both of which shared a corporate identity with the Minx series. An attractive feature was the two-tone paintwork, which helped highlight the car's modified profile; moreover, adoption of full-width body styling actually reduced the overall vehicle width by 1¼in to 5ft 3¼in, though the internal dimensions were actually increased.

Customers of the new model Husky quickly appreciated the car's quieter running and more compliant suspension, added to which it was possible to raise the maximum cruising speed to 65mph. There was also some consolation in that the de-tuned Minx engine, with its lowered compression ratio and smaller carburettor venturi, was designed to run on cheaper low-grade fuel.

Economies remained in respect of the car's interior specification: whilst the driver's seat continued to have limited fore and aft adjustment, thus compromising the comfort of long-legged drivers, movement of the front passenger seat was restricted to being tilted forward in order to afford access to the rear compartment. Simplicity was not restricted to the interior trimming; facia design and instrumentation were elementary, as were the external button and hook door catches and handles, which, nonetheless, were exceptionally efficient in use. Converting the Husky into a load carrier by folding the rear seats to form a flat floor called for minimal effort. Even with the rear seats raised there was adequate stowage space, while the spare wheel and tools were stowed for quick access beneath the load platform immediately in front of the tailgate opening.

A Series II Husky was introduced in March 1960 to feature a deeper front windscreen along with a roof line that was lowered by 1½in. Inside the car the appointments were slightly more luxurious than before. Improved seating added to comfort and, mechanically, the model was enhanced in August 1960 with a hypoid rear axle.

The Husky underwent its final, and perhaps most significant, incarnation in August 1963 when Rootes unveiled the firm's 1964 models. The most sophisticated Husky yet displayed the latest corporate Minx frontal styling along with a lowered bonnet line. In nearly 10 years the little Hillman had progressed from what could essentially be described as a van conversion to a purpose-built small family hatchback having all the comforts of a modern saloon combined with the versatility of an estate car.

When fitted to the Series III Husky, the Minx's 1,390cc power unit was modified to provide peak power of 40.5bhp at 4,200rpm. However, when specified for the American market, the Husky sported the Minx's 1,592cc engine.

Though displaying a measure of austerity, the interior of the Series III Husky was decidedly luxurious compared to earlier models. The flooring material, in the form of ribbed rubber carpeting, was designed to be removed for cleaning, but the covering to the gearbox and transmission hump was rubber-faced felt and therefore all the more coarse. The front and rear seats were far more substantial than before but, again, only the driver's seat was adjustable for fore and aft movement, while simplistic styling meant the continued use of plain plastic interior door panels, which, despite their soberness, were quite easy to clean. The instrumentation, now housed in twin dials within the grey-painted metal facia ahead of the driver, was not only modern in appearance but, for a small utility car, surprisingly comprehensive. Available as genuine Rootes' aftermarket accessories were oil pressure and coolant temperature gauges that could also be fitted to the Minx.

The equipment list, albeit most of it optional, made for inspiring reading. It wasn't all what it seemed, however, especially as the fresh-air heater, a non-

The Husky received a new image in 1960 with a modified roofline, deeper windscreen, new-style radiator grille and new body panels. Added to the recipe were more comfortable seats and improved interior heating. *Rootes publicity/Alan Earnshaw collection*

The Series III Husky, as pictured, featured a lower bonnet line and modified radiator grille in keeping with then current Minx styling. Under the bonnet there was a detuned 1,390cc overhead-valve engine that was uprated to 1,592cc for the North American market. *Rootes publicity/author's collection*

standard item, was lethargic in operation, even with the booster fan working. The cold air ventilator, boosted by the same fan, came in for some criticism by *Autocar's* road tester, along with the virtually inaudible horn.

On the plus side, customers praised the new generation Husky for light and precise steering as well as its 34ft plus turning circle. Conversion of the interior for load-carrying purposes remained a strong feature, but the side-hinged tailgate, which could only be opened from outside the vehicle, would have been more useful had it been reconfigured as either top hinged or split horizontally.

Performance-wise, the Series III Husky was ideally suited to hard work, even if acceleration could be described as being leisurely. The car's maximum speed was around 75mph, even with a full load, and gear changing was precise courtesy of the stubby gear lever. Possibly Rootes' marketing team missed a trick by not specifying the Husky with the 1,600 engine and all-synchromesh gearbox reserved for USA export models.

The Husky remained in production until the end of 1965, by which time minor mechanical revisions included a front anti-roll bar from late in 1964, recirculating-ball steering to replace the worm-and-nut arrangement, and adoption of 5.60x15 tyres instead of the previous 5.00x15 types.

For years the Husky was a familiar sight on British roads and renowned for its rugged engineering and longevity. Though the Husky name was to disappear, it was reincarnated in 1967 as an addition to the Hillman Imp range of vehicles.

The Imp

Billy and Reggie Rootes knew only too well that the Hillman catalogue lacked a car smaller than the Husky but which nevertheless enjoyed the attributes of Fiat's 600, Renault's 4CV and the VW Beetle. The latter became a constant reminder to Billy Rootes of a missed opportunity especially as he had been the architect of a disparaging report about the car and proclaiming it would never sell. The brothers were all too aware of small car developments in Europe that were to evolve into the likes of the Daf, NSU and Trabant, while from Japan, there emerged Daihatsu, Honda and Subaru. Then there was BMC's Mini that had achieved iconic status and made small cars highly fashionable.

Rootes began developing a small car project in the late 1950s, the exercise being carried on under the utmost secrecy. Under wraps were proposals that, had they materialised, would have matured to reveal a diminutive vehicle with bubble-car characteristics, the styling emphasis being on the streamline profile much in way of the Goggomobil and Maico. Not convinced that this was the way forward, the concept was given over to the company's design team, principally two young engineers, Mike Parkes and Tim Fry.

Taking responsibility for developing what was known as the Apex project, Parkes and Fry abandoned all previous styling ideas. They settled upon unitary construction and angular full-width body shape, the features of which displayed a flat stubby bonnet, narrow roof line and notched tail. In order to give the illusion of the car being bigger than it was, it was decided to position the headlamps as wide apart as was possible and treat the tail lamps in similar vein. The size of the vehicle dictated it to have two doors, though the plan was for it to be a full four-seater.

The Apex project took its cue from an earlier period in the company's history when plans to build a small car emerged in 1938 in the form of a creation known

Imps seen under production at Linwood, a factory where many of the manual workers were ex-shipbuilders more accustomed to heavy industry rather than car building. Linwood was known for its difficult worker-management relationship; this was one reason why production never reached the targets anticipated by the company. *Rootes publicity/Alan Earnshaw collection*

Being built in Scotland, there is little surprise that some of the Imp publicity photographs were specially taken with the Forth Bridge as a backdrop. In this picture, the compact dimensions of the Imp are clearly evident, the headlamps and taillights deliberately being located so as to make the car look wider than it was. *Rootes publicity/Alan Earnshaw collection*

Discussions concerning a baby Hillman had been ongoing since 1938 with a project known as Little Jim. The subject was again addressed some time before the launch of BMC's Mini in 1959, design work having been conducted in secrecy through two young engineers, Mike Parkes and Tim Fry. Ideas progressed around a tiny experimental car called the Slug but were ultimately dropped in favour of an altogether more conventional idea known as the Apex. Here the Slug, with its rounded features and rear-mounted twin-cylinder air-cooled horizontally-opposed engine, is seen in the Rootes design studio.
Rootes publicity/Alan Earnshaw collection

as Little Jim, which shared certain styling issues with the Standard Eight. Unsuccessful as Little Jim development was, a further attempt was made to produce a minicar in 1949 or thereabouts. This was the minuscule Slug with its rear-mounted twin-cylinder, horizontally-opposed air-cooled engine and an interior that was not unlike that of a Citroën 2CV. Parkes and Fry tried to develop the little oddity with its strange handling characteristics and drove it with zest while they experimented with an altogether new design that was destined to become the Imp.

Whereas Alec Issigonis boldly adopted front-wheel drive for the Mini, it was a rear-engine configuration that was chosen for Hillman. Peter Ware, chief executive engineer at Rootes, decided that such a format with a featherweight engine would result in a near ideal weight distribution, afford light and precise steering, as well as providing exceptional traction when negotiating steep gradients and slippery conditions. Other factors considered were even distribution of braking and equal tyre wear between front and rear wheels, both of which would have been absent in front-wheel drive and front-engine/rear-drive layouts.

Left: Fashion dictated an angular shape for the small Hillman, which was taken up by Mike Parkes and Tim Fry working under Ted White's direction. Here an experimental Imp is seen undergoing the very necessary crash testing. *Rootes publicity/Alan Earnshaw collection*

Bottom Left: From the outset of production the Imp caught the attention of the motor sport fraternity. This 1966 example is seen competing in England's Lake District almost 30 years later. *Author*

Bottom Right: With its engine and gearbox neatly located in the tail, the Imp had a spacious interior which was enhanced with the rear seats laid flat to afford a capacious carrying space. The young ladies pictured here with a fleet are evidently delighted at the thought of driving away in their brand new cars. *Rootes publicity/Alan Earnshaw collection*

The engine for what became the Imp was developed in collaboration with Coventry Climax and displayed a number of advanced features. As a result of the all-aluminium 875cc engine being considerably lighter in weight than a comparable cast-iron unit, it not only promised admirable economy, the overhead camshaft combined with a high compression ratio of 10:1 pledged outstanding performance. All the more exciting for Rootes' management was the fact that the Imp would be the first large-scale British production car to feature an all-aluminium OHC engine.

Work undertaken on the Imp's independent all-round suspension, with coil springs and swing axles at the front and coil springs with semi-trailing single wishbones at the rear, meant that the design offered superb road holding characteristics. When subjected to extreme test conditions, the prototype vehicle demonstrated its ability to corner with degrees of surefootedness unlikely to be found even with the most potent sports cars.

Although, development of the Imp had seemed to be markedly positive, there were, nevertheless, serious problems. A new factory was needed in which to build

Right: Style and comfort with real 40-45mpg economy was the message proclaimed by Rootes in its advertising for the Imp. Illustrated here is a Mark II version. *Rootes publicity/author's collection*

Bottom Left: Despite its rear-engine layout and tail-heavy design, the Imp performed well as a result of its rack-and-pinion steering and the independent all-round suspension being cleverly configured. During the course of production several improvements were made to the Imp's specification, with the result that a Series 2 was introduced in 1968. With the Imp 3 came a better-equipped interior. *Author*

Bottom Right: Badge engineering meant that the Imp was also marketed as a Singer and Sunbeam, both having an improved specification over the more basic Hillman model. The Super Imp, a late model as seen here, featured wide-rim wheels and was designed to offer customers a car featuring a higher level of appointment. *Rootes publicity/Alan Earnshaw collection*

The frontal styling of this Super Imp identifies it as Mk III with its improved appointment. Earlier Super Imps were criticised for their front seats, which were said to be too small and lacked adequate adjustment for tall drivers. *Rootes publicity/Alan Earnshaw collection*

the car and, had the Rootes brothers had their way, this would have been sited in Coventry adjacent to the existing works. The government of the day, however, wanted large scale manufacturing to be undertaken in what was termed 'designated development areas', one being Linwood near Glasgow. After much deliberation Linwood was chosen, on a site neighbouring one of Pressed Steel's factories.

Not only was Linwood expensive to build, at £22m, industrial relations dogged the factory to the extent that car production failed to meet the anticipated potential. Much of the problem arose because the local workforce had little experience in mass-production methods that were in operation elsewhere in the motor industry. Linwood was a shipbuilding area with dedicated working practices and the move to an entirely different regime presented difficulties that both workforce and management were unable to resolve.

Though it was announced in 1960 that the Imp would be produced in Scotland, production of the car did not get under way until May 1963, by which time the Mini, launched in August 1959, had succeeded in making an unstoppable impact on both the British and international motor markets.

Despite the Imp performing well in staged demonstrations, there remained a number of reliability issues that proved difficult to resolve at the time of its launch. Water pumps were unreliable, the 'lubed for life' king pins had a habit of seizing and there were various transmission faults along with pneumatic throttle failures and automatic choke maladies. Overall, though, the Imp was a spirited little car that was too often underrated. A more fundamental issue was the advanced engine die-casting plant that presented the majority of problems for which there were too few specialist engineers at Rootes to address.

Complications that have been described were not apparent in the encouraging road tests that were published at the time of the car's launch. Even the price of the de Luxe Imp at £532, which was £39 more expensive than the equivalent Mini, wasn't seen as a disadvantage.

A 'sporting' version of the Imp was introduced in 1967 under the guise of the Californian. Smart looking, with its fastback body styling, and chic, with its fully reclining front seats and lowered steering column, sales of the car lost out to the Sunbeam Stiletto. *Rootes publicity/Alan Earnshaw collection*

The Imp remained in production until 1976 by which time 440,032 examples had been constructed, a figure falling well short of that anticipated by Rootes. Seen here is the power pack assembly line at Linwood. *Rootes publicity/Alan Earnshaw collection*

The clever design of the Imp accommodated four adults in comfort and five at a squeeze, criticism being confined to the front seat cushions, which, for tall drivers, restricted the amount of thigh support. Visibility through the deep windscreen and side windows was excellent compared to many cars at the time, a feature enhanced by the slender roof pillars. The Imp design team had taken some styling cues from the Mini, hence the useful door and quarter pockets. Plus points were winding windows and opening quarterlights, neither of which featured on the Mini. The position of the engine, which was steeply canted in order for it to lie beneath the rear luggage compartment, not only meant that the drive train took up the minimum of space but also that the rear seat squab, when folded, allowed for an impressive amount of baggage area. A novel idea was the opening rear-window hatch through which to load and unload items and, of course, having a rear-mounted engine meant that the front compartment served as useful stowage space in addition to housing the spare wheel.

The Imp's handling and performance prompted one road tester to comment that it was possible to hurl the car into corners at speeds that, on other cars, would be suicidal. Then there was the innovative pneumatic throttle link providing the most sensitive control but, which, because it became problematic and tiresome when driving in heavy traffic, was later replaced by a conventional cable arrangement. There was also precise rack-and-pinion steering and a near neutral steering characteristic. The most outstanding traits of the car's handling qualities were the absence of body roll and tyre squeal when cornering. That the car handled particularly well at speed on winding roads

Often said to be the best of the Imps was the Husky, Hillman's smallest estate car being introduced in 1967. This, the third generation Husky, featured a superb carrying capacity. Chrysler had already acquired Hillman when the Husky made its debut, which is why the model remained in production for no more than three years. *Rootes publicity/Alan Earnshaw collection*

The Imp-derived Husky was a difficult car to make as a result of its body design and the fact that the load floor was raised above the engine and transmission. For customers of the Husky the one-piece lift-up tailgate was a boon, as was the 25cu ft luggage capacity. *Rootes publicity/Alan Earnshaw collection*

and that a measure of understeer was achieved were attributable to counteracting the weight bias over the rear wheels by the adoption of a wide difference between front and rear tyre pressures, those at the front having 15psi, the rear 30.

The all-synchromesh transmission came in for universal praise, again a road tester describing it as the best yet experienced. The all-round drum brakes, too, proved to be more than adequate for a car of such performance potential and, overall, the Imp showed itself to characterise a genre of small vehicle: the supermini.

Notwithstanding the Imp's surefootedness, the Hillman was viewed as being somewhat unfashionable especially as the universal trend towards front-wheel drive had been given a substantial boost by the Mini's rallying prowess.

Some 18 months after its launch, the Imp underwent some tidying and engine tweaking, the opportunity being taken to update the catalogue, resulting in the Mk II. In September 1965 the Hillman Super Imp was introduced, the 875cc engine remained but now developed 39bhp at 5,000rpm by having slightly larger valves and a manual choke. Other modifications included wheels having 4½in rims instead of the previous 4in type, improved sound proofing and restyled seats with improved cushions and contoured squabs.

The Super Imp was in fact a model that was half-way between the Mk II Imp and the upmarket Singer Chamois, badge-engineering also resulted in the sporty Sunbeam Stiletto. The accent was on refinement that included a styling makeover to allow for a dummy radiator grille at the front, decorative side strips, special wheel trims and dedicated Super Imp emblems at the front and rear as well as on the rear pillars.

The Imp range received a stylish addition in January 1967 with the arrival of the Californian that was essentially a fastback design. Costing £71 more than the Super Imp, revisions, in addition to the new body shape, amounted to provision of reclining front split rear seats. The useful rear hatch facility was lost in the body makeover and, though the Imp's excellent luggage capacity was unaltered, the seating, generally, lacked necessary support and adjustment.

The interior of the Imp, which, in this case, is a post-Mark II Super Imp with the dashboard design afforded to the later models. Earlier Imps had fluted style seats while attempts were made at giving cars floral pattern upholstery in keeping with the Swinging Sixties and Flower power. *Rootes publicity/Alan Earnshaw collection*

Another version of the Imp to appear was the Husky estate car, which was introduced in 1967 and which was derived from the Commer Imp van introduced three years earlier. The Husky was a difficult car to produce, mainly because of having its load floor constructed above the engine compartment. The front of the car, up to the front doors, was standard Imp while the rear section was given a one-piece lift-up tailgate accessing the 25cu ft cargo area. The Husky inherited the Imp's handling characteristics, which were improved with specification of radial ply tyres, the first Imp to be so equipped; it went out of production in 1970.

When Rootes decided to introduce a small car a number of design parameters were considered. The car that emerged in 1963 was expected to sell in large numbers with the intention of rivalling BMC's Mini, which it failed to do. Instead of having front-wheel drive, the car was designed with a rear-engine layout. Despite being, therefore, tail heavy, the Imp displayed surprisingly impressive roadholding characteristics, which led the car to be successfully promoted in motor sport. *Author*

The Hillman Imp is popular among classic car enthusiasts and a number remain to afford excellent service, whether used on a regular basis or kept for rallies and shows. *Author*

As soon as the Imp was launched the car found favour with the motor sport fraternity. Before long Imps were turning up at different rallies to win awards and, generally, to acquire a reputation for reliability and performance. The car was, nevertheless, underpowered for out and out sporting purposes and, for 1965, the company's engineers, in collaboration with the firm's Competition Department, produced an engine bored out to 998cc for the Rallye model.

Before that, a number of tuners worked on the Imp to develop further the engine, which, because of its design, proved not to be easy. Nerus had produced a conversion to extract more power, after which Moto Baldet marketed an Imp body styling kit to feature, among other items, modified bumpers and a twin headlamp conversion. Roger Nathan Tuning also got to work by producing an engine modification that increased the capacity to 998cc. For owners wishing to customise their Imps, Rootes approved a number of accessories including sun roofs, rally seats, alloy wheels, sports-style steering wheels, Koni shock absorbers and Kenlowe Airomatic fans.

Rosemary Smith and Valerie Domleo, driving one of two Rootes 998cc Imps, entered the 1965 Tulip Rally and stormed to victory, achieving an outright win, the Grand Touring Category and the Coupe des Dames. In second place, in the other Imp, were 'Tiny' Lewis and Dave Pollard, the combined success fairly and squarely putting Hillman in the international spotlight. The same year saw Rootes excel in the RAC Rally with the 998cc Imp taking the much coveted team prize.

Rootes produced an official sports version of the car that was marketed as the Rallye Imp. Unfinished cars were sent from Linwood to the Rootes Competition Department at Coventry where they were fitted with beefed-up suspension systems, specially designed facias and instrumentation, servo braking and high performance 998cc engines delivering 60bhp (which was 5bhp more than a standard Mini Cooper of identical capacity) at 6,200rpm to provide top speed of 92mph.

The Imp enjoyed a particularly successful racing and rallying career, the car becoming a regular competitor at major events. Tuners and competitors alike devised various ways of deriving even greater levels of performance from their cars and it was not unusual to find Imps producing more than 100bhp, though such cars were unlikely to be seen driven under normal road conditions.

During the 13 years the Imp and its derivatives were built, production accounted for 440,032 vehicles, a figure that was substantially fewer than originally had been expected. In its most productive year no more than 29,000 Imps were delivered, the figure being a far cry from the 90,000 that Rootes had anticipated selling annually.

Billy Rootes is recorded admiring the Imp, in this instance a Sunbeam, on one of his visits to America. Accompanied here by the actor Cary Grant, Billy never missed an opportunity to publicise the Rootes' empire, a business, which, for so many years, was central to Britain's motor industry. *Rootes publicity/Alan Earnshaw collection*

The Arrow Era

THERE was a new direction for Hillman in the 1960 when, in June 1964, Chrysler took a large stake in Rootes. Development of new models began; this evolved into the Arrow project that resulted in relatively staid designs, the first to appear being the Hillman Hunter in October 1966.

The Arrow project encompassed the entire Rootes/Chrysler range and, from the outset, was never intended as being anything other than wholly conventional. Leading the design was Rootes' man Rex Fleming, who produced a vehicle profile that was modern even if it was at times described as being uninspiring. For a lot of British motorists this is exactly what they wanted, which meant that the Hunter was quickly joined by a similarly shaped Minx. The Arrow project not only produced a range of cars that clearly rivalled the Ford Cortina, which had also been introduced in 1966, it also allowed for badge engineering, proffering different levels of trim appointment along with a variety of engines and power outputs.

A new range of Hillmans was introduced after Chrysler's acquisition of Rootes. The 'Arrow' cars, as they were known, were created by Rootes' designer Rex Fleming. The first to appear was the Hunter in October 1966. Styling of the Arrow models was restrained but they were well received by customers even if the motoring media were not as always complimentary. *Rootes publicity/author's collection*

Seen at a Scottish Rootes Enthusiasts meeting at Moffat is this 1974 Avenger GLS. Unlike earlier Avengers, which had rectangular headlights, the later GL and GLS models were provided with twin circular lights. The last Avengers were badges as Talbots after Peugeot's acquisition of Chrysler's European operations. *Author*

The Minx followed the Hunter and was provided with less exterior and interior trim. An early Minx is seen here undergoing inspection at the Barlby Road Service Centre. *Rootes publicity/Alan Earnshaw collection*

The way to sell new cars was to have them photographed with attractive young ladies. Hillman, by this time under Chrysler ownership, lost no time in publicising the New Minx, as it was usually referred, in the traditional manner. *National Motor Museum*

Under the skin, the Hillman Hunter saloon was furnished with late specification Minx and Super Minx engines (1,496 and 1,725cc) and transmissions. A Hunter estate car joined the model line-up for 1970 and, at the same time, the Hunter GT took its bow. Hunters were in production between 1966 and 1977, during which time some 470,000 examples of all Hunter/Minx family vehicles had left production lines at Ryton-on-Dunsmore and Linwood.

The Arrow Hillman Minx made its debut in 1967 and looked identical to the Hunter, though close examination revealed simpler wheel trims and an absence of bumper overriders. Like its sibling, it shared a wheelbase of 8ft 2.5in, independent front suspension, coil springs, Macpherson struts and front disc and rear drum brakes. The Minx was fitted with the Hunter's 1,496cc engine though automatic versions received the larger unit. The Minx name was retained until 1970 when it was dropped in favour of the Hunter DL. Hillman customers had already seen the Minx name disappear on the estate car, which was simply known as the Hillman Estate, and felt aggrieved at the Minx appellation being dropped after a run of 38 years.

A new Hillman appeared in 1970 in the guise of the Avenger. Again this was a pure Rootes' design but it did not follow the Arrow styling. Instead it was smaller and shapelier than the Minx and Hunter, being intended to rival the Morris Marina, Vauxhall Viva and Ford Escort. Unlike the Arrow cars, which shared a great many components, the Avenger had virtually nothing in common with other Hillmans, Singers or Sunbeams. It had a unique chassis and was built as two- and four-door saloons in addition to a five-door estate car, all having an 8ft 2inch wheelbase. The first Avenger to appear was the four-door, followed by the two-door and finally the estate car.

The Minx estate car was never so called as a result of the gradual dropping of the Minx name. The Hillman estate car, as it was marketed, had a generous interior capacity, which made it popular with customers. *Rootes publicity/Alan Earnshaw collection*

The engine range of the Avenger comprised a 1,248cc affair along with a 1,295cc unit. Upscale was a 1,498cc engine and a 1,599cc. Standard was a four-speed gearbox though a three-speed and later four-speed Borg-Warner auto was available. Badged as a Hillman, the Avenger was in production until 1976, after which it wore Chrysler decals until 1979 when it became a Talbot until its demise in 1981. Production of all types of Avenger numbered 638,631 cars.

Chrysler's fortunes in the late 1970s were dire and, in 1978, its European operation was sold to Peugeot. The Talbot name was gracing Rootes/Chrysler cars within a year and, before another three years were out, the entire Rootes' establishment was being dismantled. First to go was Linwood after which Ryton-on-Dunsmore became a Peugeot assembly plant and has since closed. Today, Peugeot's offices at Pinley House in Coventry overlook a housing estate where once stood the Humber factory.

Index